THE POWER OF THE TELLING

THE POWER OF THE TELLING

COLLECTED POEMS

DAVID HATHWELL

Arc Light Books

Published by Arc Light Books

Cover and book design by Jan Camp

ISBN: 978-1-939353-36-8

Cover photo of *Verbena hastata* (blue vervain)
by R. A. Nonenmacher, Wikimedia Commons CC-BY-SA 4.0

Author photo by Audrey Chavez

For my students

CONTENTS

PREFATORY NOTE

The fifty poems collected here were written within a span of about ten years, beginning in 2008, the year I retired from English teaching. Only after retiring was I free to write poetry in earnest—no responsible high-school English teacher is spared creative energies for personal use. But it was through teaching good poetry to good students that I came to feel privy to the secrets of poetic expression and able, finally, to attempt contributions of my own to its remarkable traditions.

Unusually for a poetry collection, the notes about the poems are extensive, in length and number; all the poems have them. They remain supplementary—to be consulted after reading a poem (or ignored altogether).

1. WONDER

When Musicians Applaud

When musicians applaud, they do the oddest thing.
To praise the command of the maestro,
Or the skill of another member of the ranks,
These masters of music and decorum—
Masters of movement in time—
Abandon all art to pound their feet
Against the soundboard of the stage.

Nothing civil now. Close by—in the next hall—
A band of rebels tramples the palace floor,
Mouths mute for stealth, weapons raised;
Or farther off, in the shadows of a forest haunt,
The gathered pack beats bark, drum, and gourd
To celebrate the kill—no rise to a climax
Then decrescendo, no easing to a cadence,
Just explosive start and stop.

It must be that they still are as they were,
Before melody was added, and room for silence,
And the power found in the single beat
To marshal breath and muscle, joint and limb
In the making of a long, shaped, concerted sound.

Recalled to their task, the forces rally now—
Hang poised within their ranks until, at the signal
From the leader, they raise their instruments again
And together celebrate beauty.

Fred's Girl

Astaire's partners are never anywhere as good. But sometimes better.
—Jeff Escoffier, dance writer, in conversation

Truant Muse master, would-be mortal,
Apollo on his strolling visit fumbled
his disguise—the old, ageless rubber mask
and high extraplanetary chic ("Astaire"!),
sleeves to gloves, slacks to pumps
to hide the lineaments of deity;
the sprung displays of purest energy
neither gathered nor renewed,
in succeeding gestures earthward—
blasts of rat-tat tapping syncopation—
or released into the air without the weight
of gravity, each crowned and brightly
finished, all rounded and complete;
then the signs by which we mortals
know him best: radiance, serenity.

But Ginger, Joan, Rita, Paulette—
creatures of flesh no doubt. Standing,
at first, coltishly uncertain, in time
coaxed forward by the master to try
her untried limbs, each submits her being
to test on test of line and balance—
bends and dips, easy turns then whipped
and spun, leaps and prancing shuffles,
struts urged to gallops, lunges held,
reversed, at full, half, double speed.

Blood racing—breathless, gleaming—
she dances with her own, ideal image,
but he, with godly gallantry, bids us
watch the girl, *delight in her,* shows us
not their distance but her unlikely brave
advances, her thrilling proximity.

Flesh so near to spirit, she exults.
In her joy she wants to laugh, exclaim,
but the momentum of these movements
has her, pulls her, lifts her onward, up.
This is close to heaven—what could
ever be as good? She's Fred's girl,
she's in heaven, she can hardly speak.

Poplar

Surely this one is meant for our delight—
When, hidden in the green, a hundred butterflies,
Catching a breeze, flutter sage and silver wings
In tethered flight—or a dozen veiled limbs,
Lifting in the wind, swing their lavish weave
Of flashing bangle, leaf, and twig coyly
In and out of sight.

Hard, that is, to see within the lovely show
Economies of growth, accommodated
Circumstance—to recognize the play of leaf
And branch, the rich invention of their repertoire,
As strategies devised by chance to ease
The take of air and light.

For pleasure freely taken, all due thanks—
Applaud the accidental show. All honor
To the spectacle—clearest to the nourished eye—
Of gratifying need: the appetite for abundance,
The will to sense and feed.

Red Dress

Two gold bands,
nestled matrimonially
against a soft blue field,
offer the fine symmetry
of twinned circles burnished
to an even glow. The page
frames them brilliantly—
reachably distant and still—
for the admiring eye.

Elsewhere, emerging from
an evening crowd, a lovely dress—
luxe geometries of line and
curve alive in movement,
its rich red many reds—
gathers light and lifts from the page.
Its ruby radiance fills to the brim—
fills to overflowing and fills and fills.
It becomes Red Dress, wins all
red dresses to its glorious form—
the only one and all you need.

The Day the Spaceship Landed

When the ship touched down
no better than thirty feet away,
she was holding her favorite cup
at the kitchen window.

"Peach tree," she said—
at a rare loss for words.
"It's the tree hit by lightning
all over again."

But that wasn't it, she knew.
Yielding, she stood and stared,
for the moment speechless,
alone facing wonder,

until she recognized—yes!—
a giant, face-down lily,
big as the coffee cup "sculpture"
good for a laugh in Moon Park,

the altar kind, just the flower,
silky white on a bugle curve,
with the lovely long bridal pleats
and hoop of flaring petals,

somehow installed, in the hot light
of an August afternoon
while the lazy dozed,
in the middle of her own backyard.

She imagined nubbly creatures
joined by curling filaments,
piping in their alien language
the excitement of the mission—

whose purpose she was fated
not to know. Before her eyes
the lily landed silently again,
backwards—rose a yard or so,

hovered (a dainty lampshade?),
revved to a whirling spin,
then leapt lightly skyward,
traceless in the grass and gravel.

Again master of her world,
she turned and padded off,
cup in hand, to check the wash.
It was all up to her.

She had her anecdote,
and would wield her ready words
to hold their ears and dumb, rapt faces
until they believed it.

2. POINTS OF VIEW

Hit the Deer

How did he die?
Suddenly and quick,
the police say.
To miss the deer
he swerved,

then swerved again
too soon, skidded,
flipped, and rolled—
tracks like these
are fairly common
on this road.

On the highway headed home,
at one a.m., mercifully alone.

What he might have,
should have done:
the mind would like
to ask but can't,
blocked, at every turn,
by what he merely did.

The image of the deer
—exposed and taut,
baffled, will-less,
caught by the unknown—
was his own.

Shipwreck

Last night I sank a ship.
Down it went. Just like that.

A trim little liner fitted
for fun, decked and bannered

like a shiny model on a pond
suddenly shoved downward,

fighting for buoyancy
while its chambers flood

until, unresisting, down it goes.

*

Though, remembering now,
I suppose I merely watched.

It must have been some injury
to the hull, but looked as if

the open sky, heavy with
the leaden blue of dawn,

had simply pressed its weight
against the open sea

to make a greater emptiness.

*

A dozen baffled gulls
circling invisible perches

flew wider and wider until
the sun rose up and absorbed

them into its terrific light.

Readiness Is Everything

Always be ready.
—Matthew 24.42

Imagine the world without you
and you're nearly there. The Spanish Steps
in early September, for instance,
its extravagant expanses—"widest in the world"—
under the church towers' disapproving gaze.

Tourists and locals dispose themselves
as they always do on a vivid late-summer afternoon.
To the right, among the idle seated
under the bright Roman sky—an isle of stillness—
a young visitor, standing, eagerly explores
the death of Keats (where exactly? when
and how?), eyes in a well-worn guide book.
On the quiet bank just across, another traveler,
this one a student of the present, leans back
on bare elbows, tilting his head,
in the resonant air, to receive all he can
of the life of the piazza, of Rome and Italy
and the wider world, while passing citizens
walk their steps in streams of traffic
flowing up and down the center.

Oddly, the scene is silent.
But this is a memento, a postcard from the past.
I am that earnest student of the past—
the Kodak on a strap his own historian—
just as I am the traveler with his eyes closed,

venturing forth, at his bravest, with the uncertain
rhythms of blind eagerness. The vantage point
and form and frame—mine again—
bring these single figures, equal yet opposed,
into easy focus, survivors on safe shores
beside the swirling crosscurrents of rushing
passersby. A commanding perspective—
the reach of its converging diagonals—
secures a lovely order, though the horizon
and vanishing point can't be seen.

Sunday at the Symphony

Again, in the dimmed assembly hall
ready as a church for ritual, an evening
exhibition of spectral warhorses:
a Something Suite after an overture
to nothing, a long, lulling ride on
a phantom gondola, before intermission
a masterly seascape deemed the best.

To recover ourselves, we stand, seek
bright cleared spaces, regroup or roam.

Next a young Polish (Finnish?) violin
with an accomplished, quiet bearing
and Tchaikovsky's grand concerto,
plush reliquary of fine feeling,
so wan its gestures, so feeble its hold
on the heart its first devotees must
have been ghosts, summoned tonight
to this convocation of pale spirits.

Dust Is Winning

Go to a shelf.
With an index finger
touch the top of the spine
of a book, any book,
and tilt the book
toward you. Blow.
Caught in its indifference
it scatters, riding the blast,
till, weighted by inertia,
it sinks and settles,
invisible again.

Under cover of invisibility
it steals everywhere,
takes hold on horizontals
and, somehow, verticals,
squatter above and below,
outside and in.
No wonder, then, its ease on air.
Inhale and in it goes—
out just CO_2—its residue
a fine, filmy mud
we make our own.
(Cough, if you'd like.)

All we do is make ready—
    pull the covers,
    rinse the dish
    and wipe the counter,
    seal the windows,
    secure the door—
so that now, the field cleared,
    without strategy
    or even intent,
    unseen and unheard
    it advances,
    drifts and spreads,
    in the thickening stillness
    reclaims its own
    by falling to rest.

Schadenfreude

n.f. Willowherb: any plant of the genus *Epilobium* of the evening-primrose variety; *esp.* fireweed: a tall perennial having terminal spiking clusters of pinkish-purple flowers, their nectar-rich centers an important source of honey in some areas; known as rosebay in the United Kingdom and bombweed in Great Britain, owing to its rapid colonization of ground burned by the blitz, flourishing near wreckage and in its interstices and bringing bright bursts of color to sites otherwise grim [*fr. Schaden* damage + *Freude* joy].

Allan Gardens

Central Toronto, Ontario

Safer lost
in two dimensions,

supple tail
seizing to an *S*,
the squirrel moves

by fits and stops

through states of
stillness snapped

from shot
to shot.

During Restless Sleep a Scene of Remarkable Stillness

On the far side of a river,
holly lines the riverbank.
The leaves are lacquered tiles.

In the distance, along the horizon,
giant cypresses, all indigo, link
their lower limbs.

Between, a field of grass
rolls unbroken
in suspended waves.

The pond, or lake—too still
to be a river—is a better blue
than the unmarked sky.

Within its deep painterly glow
the holly hangs in amethyst clusters,
and it brims.

Nothing moves. No breeze
touches a branch or leaf
or plays over the meadow.

Lake, brush, grass, and trees
hold their line and color
under the sun's probing light.

Nothing stirs in the hidden depths
to make the water ripple, or spill
beyond its borders into the land.

Messenger

Look! Morning has begun and yet the moon—
there, above the horizon—the moon isn't fading!

The sky's its liquid blue,
a few low bands of cloud
hold their paling orange
in almost-breaking waves—
and there, by some trick
of light, hangs a bright full moon—

against a pastel wash the hard impasto,
white, gray, and black, of its spotted sphere.

Good-bye seems wrong,
so does good morning,
at this odd conjunction
of our world of every day and beyond—

where, seen or unseen, all moving bodies
roll and spin, in locking circuits weave,
rotate, and revolve, in darkness or in light,
at blind, contending forces' strict commands.

Follower of the Laws of Motion,
for the moment messenger,
this bright moon seems to say
that there is no difference
between the beginning of our day and night.

Through My Window

If we had a keen vision and feeling of all ordinary human life . . .
—George Eliot, *Middlemarch*

Behind the spare proscenium of the frame
a woman enters, stage right, on a beeline to stage left.
Groomed for business, striding eyes forward,
she cannot see, as she swerves to miss,
the young man just appearing upstage center,
through the double doors of a café storefront
not, I recall, a scrim.

His sight trained equally on what lies ahead,
he hauls a strip of rubber flooring, hiked
against a hip, slowly downstage center
to his station at the curb, then takes a beat,
and drops it flush along the ledge.
Standing straight (not so young, I see),
in his clean white apron of the day,
he seems to me, as he inspects the mat
to weigh the task, to eye within its length
the prospect of the day's familiar labors
yet to come, and, as he turns to make his way
upstage and off, to trudge, with lowered sight,
a narrowed, beaten track that, truth to tell,
I'm pleased to be unable to pursue.

Stage empty, vision idling, my mind
is freed to contemplate the frame.
If all the world's a stage, who, I muse,
must be its privileged spectators?
And I start the tale of a minor Roman god,

or better still a legendary ancient king,
a king, let's say, of former Thessaly,
who, covetous of higher-powered sight,
tries to scale Olympus for the view
and then is punished for his crime,
with the gift of perfect vision
and, high upon a promontory, everlasting life.

I see, in a head bent back and away against an infinite sky,
a pair of restless wild eyes locked in striving not to see,
and hear, through the tortured mouth that crowns him now,
the long, unrelieving cries of boundless all-seeing impotence . . .

Saved from griefs so unlike my own,
I cozy back to figures on a well-framed stage
—at the moment three, poised, it seems,
on an apron for a bow, but with profiled heads,
on craned necks, turned smartly to stage left—
toward, I see, a late commuting bus looming
as if cued. Heaving dutifully under its load,
it drags to a dead stop dead center, in time
revives, and—neat little vanishing act to give
the scene a close—lumbers off an emptied stage
to only God knows where.

3. BONDS

Relativity

The bus I heard would be his, I knew,
so I stopped to face the street as it approached,
hoping (he knew my route) to catch his eye, smile, and wave.
But I saw, as the bus drew near, that he sat facing inward—
saw, passing before me and away,
in a bright light having nothing to do with the evening,
just the loose green shoulders of his jacket,
the dark band of the back of his cap,
and, between, the nape and soft patch of gray
calling again to be loved—
and the greeting I intended became a kind of good-bye.

No. It was as if we—my long companion and I—
had never met. We were traveling two paths
that for the time being ran parallel,
close enough for moments of recognition
and remembered longing but always onward,
by different means, at different speeds,
I on foot and he riding.

Orchestra, Advanced

Safe passage to character and culture
only to them, our dreaming elders.
For us, the wandering young,
fifty minutes' reprieve guaranteed
(attendance required) from the day's
grim drills of ordered aimlessness,
the weight of unsafe silences.

Having no eye for elevation,
we watched the score before us
and now and then the wagging wand
beyond, counted as we tapped out beats,
marking time until our coded cue—
then struck, bowed, plucked, or blew.
How good to be an oboe once a day.

In those rising exclamations above all,
where, from heightened watchfulness,
we looked to the truth of rhythm and
pitch, touch and timbre to mute
distinction, level difference—find
our voices in the massing sound,
knowing when to speak and how.

Voices

When I see my hand
and see my mother's hand
I hear her voice,

not words, though
she is speaking slowly,
or quietly singing,
a song half remembered
or a song of her own,

an almost-speech,
soft and finely textured
as the skin of my hand,
that lifts to a tremolo,
an easy fluttering,
of secret delight or
longing or grief,
then, wavering, fades
to a low reedy hum,

lifts and falls until, caught
by the spell of its song,
I can believe that it beckons,
that its message is for me.

Victory

How nice to think I'll see my father again,
at twenty-two or three, twenty-five at most,
at his happiest, why not,
playful and easy and wayward,
his eyes their strong, true brown,
his skin not waxen but one with his body,
still the varsity runner
ready for movement and speed.

Of course she will have to be alive to him again,
adored, more bride than mother,
at his happiest, why not.
The reunion will be as natural as daylight.
When he says "My wife" it won't be bafflement
but the reclaiming of a rightful prize,
it will be *victory.* He'll hold her again,
in a triumphant unending now.

This Week's China

Aunt Renée was expert in betrayal.
Uncle Jack stood up and swore I do
and then before you knew it
left her holding a full-grown baby
and a fat monthly debt.
But she lived and learned and life went on
until Uncle Henry—her own personal savior
and Judas all in one *ha ha*—
did just about the same—the prince
who called himself a family man
and said it was her turn now to feel like royalty.

So that settled any doubt.
Uncle Jack and Uncle Henry became
twin King Tuts in a private museum
that practically built itself—portable,
secure yet open all hours for guided tours
featuring the two old standbys
but, first, items recently acquired:
this unkept date, that unappreciated sandwich,
this unanswered prayer or phone call
(*Lean in close to take in the detail*),
that unreturned handbag, smile, friendship.

Back at the entrance, where it was time
to be reminded of the precise value
of the show, Aunt Renée's eyes—
sharp and searching then—seemed
to direct its meaning straight at me:

Look how easily a promise made
is broken—even if it's forged in steel.
Then a shrug of the shoulders and brows
to punctuate futility, and bitter final words
I loved (and silently said with her):
This week's china! . . .

Toward the end the museum closed.
On short notice Aunt Renée retired
behind grudging speech, and a blank gaze
that leveled everything before it—
us, the changing sky, rooms ever smaller,
those graying tiles and fluorescent lights—
and frightened everyone but me.

Aunt Renée, I thought, had liquidated
all her holdings, exchanged them
for a kind of song, sustaining, sounding
just for her, the music, played and shuffled
and played again, of the sudden shattering
of a bowl, the crash of bursting glass,
the rude bang of a blowout, the ripping
of a sleeve on a latch, the soft splintering
of ice beneath the feet, and—if she's lucky
(peace be with you, Aunt Renée!)—
the bright clanging of a pearly gate.

Sunflower

Grotesque cousin of the daisy,
this may be the saddest flower.
All summer, all day every day,
it lifts its wide blank face,
featureless as need, to track
the sun's slow climb across the sky.

It's a flower drawn by a child.
Penned in a vase, on single stalks,
it drops its head and moons, baffled
by the requirements of beauty.

Orphaned nightly in an open field
it hangs quiescent, left again to sleep.
Does it dream? Of course it dreams,
of an uninterrupted radiant warm
embrace beyond the need to seek.

4. THRESHOLDS

Between Dog and Wolf

There are times, at dusk,
when night has fallen
but the day won't cede,
dogs roam with the pack
and still the driver races on
with the confidence
of daylight—
                    glances back
into the closing darkness,
then locks his grip and rides
the wheel, lured by the glow
of twilight's third light
to buck danger, dodge fear.

The passengers are silent—
a breeze streams night's chill,
the blade's whir of traffic
cuts the air—
                    and still,
gunning, braced to hold
the lead, the driver plunges
headlong into shadows
lit by the eyes of wolves.

Ten O'Clock

I am too old for bedtime
and yet here it is. But now
without deep, forgiving sleep,
remission back to zero,
the next day new. And fewer
intermissions of free fantasy,
the world remade, removed.
Instead tales from life
and amply fulfilled dread.

Time again for bed. As before,
though *once more is once less,*
counting up counting down,
progression in dark increments
tending surely to zero.

Briefly, plain liminal truth,
a clear call to wakefulness
heard but not pursued.
Dull powers of reckoning,
a heavy head. Heavy lids.
The sensation of motion
slowing, under unbearable
weight, before letting go.

Waking at Seventy

It's early morning.
Or only night's end,
so empty is the stillness.
(No birds yet.)

I should be asleep
but seem to be awake.

Nothing to unsettle the silence
but the hum of rolling tires
(or is it the engine?)
rising to a crest

then falling away,
the steady arc
of long waves rolling to shore
in a slow incoming tide.

*

If I open my eyes
I'm in a vault
of corners blurring to arches
and sleeping grays.

The cool air hangs
as in a holding chamber.

If I close them
I'm under the sea
near the floor,
where light falls like shadows

and a bed of seaweed,
flickering into view,
pitches ceaselessly
between movement and rest.

Finding Myself in the Morning

The unstoppable wellspring is still.
From the next room a heaving and settling
too removed by sleep and silence
to summon, yet, his lifelong companion.

In minutes memory will seep through,
find its way in along old channels,
in its deepest reaches gather to a flow,
the past a second bloodstream pumping
into the present, speeding the pulse,
flushing the skin: his companion again,
their brother, her friend . . .

For now, I can sit alone at this table,
in this cool bright air, and trace
with slow fingers these dark veins
ambered in oak. I can hear faraway traffic
and, below, a clack of heels and silence
and something like a shout, and not wonder
who is speaking, or what comes next.

Sunday Sorrow

The piercing edge
is loss, the end
bearing down
or about to.

Home in failing
light, punctual
as the hour.
But sometimes
the early
exigent guest.

For me now
it flashes in
early morning
sightings of
the slippery
dead,

someone in
the lasting
stillness, an
old aroma,
the curve of
a spoon,

in the oak
of the kitchen
table Mother
or an aunt,

looking back
toward five
o'clock, dawn
or dusk in
her eyes,
waving or
pointing.

Gifts

Postscript to a first line from Richard Wilbur

Pronounce it good to have been born—
Dare declare this life a gift—
    If in that failing breath
    Of fast-eliding sighs
You recognize the gift of death.

5. TRANSITIONS

Sendoff

A near wreck.
Needs work
on his body
and cognition.
Thank God he's
off the road.

Though his map
isn't mine.

First a stroller
(make that
"walker"?), now
a varnished cane.
Ahead looks
relatively bright.

The best of
luck to him!

No use looking
back. Through
his rear view
you'd only see
it coming.

Slipping off the Raft

We were now at that age where some of our oldest and best friends were "slipping off the raft," as the saying goes.
—Julia Child, *My Life in France*

Welcome. You see here a classic.
All wood, the oldest sailors' way.

Fourteen logs, spruce, lashed to the frame,
the deck planed and varnished for comfort.

For ease of navigation, and to prevent homesickness,
we'll push away from the shore and make for open water.

We'll travel rivers and bays, though she's seaworthy,
and will carry us through rough currents and winds.

No risk at all of boat sickness, as we sail never against
but always with the water. We'll move as the water moves.

*

Days will be best. Especially early mornings,
when the sun is just up and the sky looks liquid too.

The horizon will trace a clean, wide arc over waters
never really settled. We'll feel the lapping against us.

We'll see birds in formations traveling their distances,
and stragglers and strays. We'll hear their calls.

If you slip and tumble into the water, we'll all laugh
as we fish you out and haul you back on board.

The clouds will make eddies of their own, and waves
that break in the flood of light at sunset.

*

Nights will take their turn. Starry nights will be fine—
we'll gasp when the skies are washed with white!

Evenings will be filled mostly by our quiet voices
mixed with the silence and the sound of lapping.

Mists and shifting banks of fog will make us wonder
what's ahead, even when we're moored for the night.

Now and then, in the still of night, one of us, shaken
by a dream, may turn restlessly and roll to the edge,

and sometimes, the edge tilting, slide over and down.
He won't reach up or cry out. He'll quietly sink.

Some of us may hear a sound, stir, and settle.
He'll think, we'll think it's only troubled sleep.

Pled from the Verge

I asked you, implored you not to let
me sink, all you had to do was face me
when I spoke, look me in the eyes,
at moments hold my arm or shoulder,
say with me what I said as I said it

but apparently I asked too much or
maybe didn't ask it clearly, it was touch
and go from the start, maybe you weren't
listening or had ideas of your own

and now look at me, look, the ground
is sand sliding under my feet, I'm on
my toes, the water's at my chest, cool
not cold, what can I do, before I know it

liftoff, I'll be floating free somewhere
on an ocean of my own, soon, you'll see,
it won't be long, I'll open my arms to
the dwindling shore, let myself go, float
far out on a cool sea facing a blank sky

and with a little effort a little more effort
I'll be silent, I won't ask at all

Pray for This

Go ahead—before it's too late—
get up—now—off your knees.
Blow out the candle. Stop the prayer,
the incessant plea, for safety, oh God,
from the unexpected—

the blast preparing its ravages
in quiet spaces below—the maw
around the corner or (who knows?)
already at the door—the thing
uncoiling beyond the wall.

Get up—while you can—and leave
this room. Walk—don't crawl.
Keep your sight line level and—
pray for this—your senses whole,
safe from sicklied hope.

If you can't—if this is all—all
is not lost. For your sake—look up
—eyes forward—past the flame
into the shadows. Contemplate—
this is important—a likely worst—

the door may slam open and in
fly a ripping torrent of peace.

I'll Be a Vessel

I'll empty myself
into the dark recesses
of its cool concavity.
I can see it: stoneware
under an ash glaze,
clean in the easy curve
of the mouth and neck
and wide, rounded shoulder,
free of ornament
and so finely shaped,
so smoothly finished that,
spinning on a sandy surface,
it would seem to stand still.

Don't think I've made room
for moans or mewlings,
the clamor of old woes,
inarticulate, bottomless.
Imagine, within, no space
for tenancy or possession,
no quarter for rending pleas,
only a quiet center locked,
for good, in shadow. Imagine
the beauty of the scene.

I'll stand, empty of memory,
under a leafy canopy,
open to intimations of sun-,
moon-, and starlight, marking
slow, diurnal rhythms,
safe from the taunts
of raw winds and rain,
claims as harmless as voices
from another room:
just a vessel, like countless
artifacts of its kind token
of another time, unobserved,
silent through centuries.

6. TELLING

The Need for Echoes

Not the canyon kind. Never those—
nature's cunning parlor trick
wherein the Maestro, all in black,
inviting exclamations from the guests,

severs—Presto!—sound from sense,
conjuring a rush of shuffled sound
that, reducing as it multiplies,

answers all our efforts to express
with a resounding *less.*

Not those, no—
rather gestures of affirmation, of assent,
the seconding reply—the nod, the *yes*—
that grants our inmost notion
—Ecco!—outward being, embodiment,

lends shadow substance, confers
upon the homeless sense of self
the sensation of a dwelling place,

and distances awhile the awful boom
of echoes of the other kind.

Reading the Fall

Watching and watching the water fall—
The wild roaring plunge chased by light—
In minutes my eyes, tired by the commotion
Of so much change and sameness, climbed up
The fall to the quieter motion at the head—

From below, just a sunken lower jaw
Edged with teeth of stones, some smoothed,
Most still cracked and angled, and spewing,
Where stone met stone or from hidden facets,
Streams and splashes into the widening fall.

A splash curled and plunged; I saw it fall,
Fall and fall in heavier, headlong slow motion—
Grand effect, I supposed, of the claim on sight
Of the time and space of its single glittering arc.
Senses quickening for a deeper vision—

Eyes again at the mouth—I caught this splash
And that and that, reaching to hold in view
Their separate, slowed descents. Reached—
And failed. Though before the blur: a glimpse into
The sources of grandeur, the falls within the fall.

* * *

The many in the one says the divining mystic,
The seer. But I am nothing of those; I am a reader,
Called by chance to read, in a privileged glimpse
Beyond the wash of first impressionism,
The hidden power of words within the word.

For watchful eyes, signal gestures—little phrases
For sounds, sights—form and mingle, each joining
The gathering force of its sure, coursing progress
To a grander spectacle of fulfillment, its cadences,
Final yet reverberant, the cadences of majesty.

Now I heard, in the roaring fall, Caddie's
Then Luster's then Dilsey's "Hush!"—saw
Willy plunge, at last, into the peaceful dark.
The bleak tidal ruckus of the bight brings
To shore its happy riot of correspondences,

Stella for falling star repeats for good
Blanche's deep descent, stone extrudes once more
To thrust the friends apart, and, borne back
On an implacable current, Gatsby reaches still
Toward flowering white-green wonder.

Song

I'm five-seven or five-eight
Depending on the day.
Mood can do that.

Sometimes I wake up
Billy Collins and the
Words seem to flow.

To shape the flow
I'm a riverbank, a weir,
The wind, the moon.

I'm a river, a sea god—
Jealous waterlord, shape
Shifter, caster of spells.

I rage against insurgents
Until, subdued, they sing
My sovereignty.

When the song is right
I'm muscled and lean
And have turnout.

I rise from my desk,
Majestic, and I dance.
Oh how I dance.

Sure Thing

You're a brick,
Yes, a hard red block that you can trust,
Unless it's accidentally cracked
Or whacked to dust.

Or rather you're a diamond,
Superbly tough and brilliant once it's ground,
Providing it's been mined
And found.

No—you're an elixir,
Whose wholesome powers to restore and mend
Magically arrest decline
Until the end.

And I? I'm a voice
That tells you what you always surely knew:
That language is prepared to lie
When you ask it to.

Do Not Use

Acacia
Alas
All day in bed intertwined
Amid
Chrysalis
Cicadas
Coruscating
Day's end
Divided soul
Dying/harsh cries/light
Edenic
Effulgent
Firmament
Flowering fields
Glimmer/glint/glisten
Indifferent blue
Lo
Long grass
Mermaid's song
Mon semblable
Mother-of-pearl
Naught
Nocturne
O
Pandora's box
Pebbled shore
Peonies
Rhythmic sigh
Sad night

Saraband
Squawking gulls
Still waters
Under the sun
Whiskey from the bottle
White wine in a mug
Widening gyre
Wind-torn
Winged beast
Wisteria
Write it!

Another Poem

Sometimes it's digging in dry dirt.
Nothing dark and loamy: dull, hard dirt.
Since you must use bare hands
your fingertips will catch fire.
They'll take the edges of stones and shards,
your treasure on a good day—
this rare button or bead,
that fine patch of rag tugging
a feather-tufted bone—
all fragments of unimaginable wholes.

No signs of life here.
What from these remnants should start—
take color—climb? Cohere and fly?

Lucky to find a worm, you'll think.
Then suddenly—oh!—
blue vervain, moonseed,
                    a leafy dragon, the snowy plover.

Family Stories

In memoriam Crecensio Cruz (1888?–1964)

Retelling his story brings
a sense of permanence.
The past isn't finished.
It's still here. Listen . . .

So she tells the story again,
to the same ears if need be,
tells it again until, in time,
by the power of the telling,

a young man named for a dead uncle
and lost in a northern land
gives way to the father,
striding visionary,

until duty yields to devotion,
doubt to bright resolve,
and the hard, broken turf
of hunch and happenstance

to open road and crossroad,
whose travel traces, at last,
the well-told tale's rise and fall,
its timeless symmetries.

Tropes

The death of death.
How fine a trope.
In a thimble
All of Christian hope.

Is it Donne's?
In wit and moment, yes,
If not in word.
He wields it best.

Show thy sting!
Armed to face a foe—
Man or thing—
Now we stand to win.

But how if death
Refuses being—
Declines the role—
Fulfilled instead
In nothingness?

Time to put the play
Of words to work
To furnish absence—
Frame the simple end—
The very death—of death.

We'll begin again.
Commemorate the dead.
Take flower, candle, song—
All that might be sung
Or said—into empty rooms.

Penned

The unstoppable,
incorruptible,
inconsolable,
uncontainable
Donald Hall
is silent.

7. APPREHENSION

The Pigeon Is a Shoe

Artful decoy at the curb,
working its spell from forty feet—
a straight-line pull across the pavement,
gait steadied by stony resignation, eyes forward.

And the pigeon is only a shoe.
Really an ankle boot, I see, the neck
folded to the toe. The leather slumps,
a dead white worn to gray along the body.

So I'm spared the memory of a bird—
on this corner, at this hour,
with or without visible injury—
and, too close, the stark look of afterlife.

Though here comes a cat from months ago,
on its side on a hearth at Guerrero
and Fourteenth, here it is among the bins,
a calico stretched out lazily in the early afternoon,
its mouth open, baring the smallest teeth,
and a split pomegranate at the neck.

Cubism

That is to say I see part of it, as of all
one sees.
—Samuel Beckett, *Malone Dies*

You can't see anything
whole, anything
entire.

Contemplate the cube:
front (or back), top
(or bottom), side,

never more than these,
more often less,
never front

and back, top and
bottom, side
and side.

To see all that you'll have
to split some half
the seams

and lay it flat. Though
there the cube's no
longer whole,

shorted of its home in
space, where we,
born prey,

must make our way
at large, wary of
what lies behind.

Geology of the Sidewalk

Once explorer of looming spaces,
now geologist of the leveled way,
I step carefully as I go, my gaze
trained downward to chart dangers
undetected by the untrained eye—
a crack opening to a crevasse,
secret slopes and sudden valleys,

gleaming stone harboring a slick
(bane of a light spring shower!),
cruel tectonic ledges and drops
too seldom scored with lines, Xs,
and Os, in bright nursery blue
or yellow, by a playful child god
relishing upheaval. Unbroken,

bent—hat tilted to a blinding sun,
coursing wind, the bounding young
(their dumb daring!)—once more
I brave the block, square by square
by square, surveying each for fresh
peril. Foolish to look forward—
dangerous to look ahead.

Hidden Force Observed

Physicists
have identified a
force, as yet unnamed,
that powerfully draws two objects
together. At last science can explain why
the common sandal clings and water seeks its own
level, why pages stick and momentum gathers. Now we know
why all lines converge except for parallels, whose bond is never broken,
why crowds assemble but the safest place is here, why the keynote once sounded,
sounded just once, seizes the ear and holds it against all comers, why there's
no place like nothing new and if it isn't one damned thing leads to
another, why before you know it a train a line a vein a flow of
thought, why where would we be without the classics,
why theories unify and the thrill of the known,
why it isn't the journey, it's the return,
why the one safe place,
why home.

Master of Shadows

Children don't go to the darkest places,
where the blind eye of the moon,
shedding a milky glow, deepens shadows,
and from the tangled margin of a forest clearing
an animal presides.

Two felid eyes—two dull moons—
say beast of prey (cougar? leopard? lynx?)
but nothing of intent, much to ask
of a forest being with knowing
in the blood.

When will it be roused again to strike?
By which rustling? shadow? scent?
Until then, it may be moved to hunt
another covert, stalk the border of another site,
or, lifting slightly, just sit silently in state,
no other way inclined.

A Suit

Time absolutely for a new one.
Aromatic wool, silk to the skin.
No plaid, no checks or stripes, God no.
Mute black, with a soft sheen
only in the fold and sway
of its cool luxury.

Handsome for the podium,
the important banquet table,
for terse but sensitive tributes
and sendoffs, ceremonious good-byes.
A seemly addition to a group
gathered by grief, shadowed
by grief, touching or holding it.
A hedge against the airless horrors
of such doings if I'm lucky.

The fit of a suit hangs
on the lay of the shoulders.
I'm ready. I'll stand up
to the clerk's best blandishments,
strong with the foresight
of its borrowed dignity.
I'll know it by its feel.

Next the hard tests of use.
The threat, for one, of faltering
newness, an ally's slow defection:
barrier, buffer, friend until,
worn by the ways of habit,
it loses the life all its own.

Start Here

The papers are just about in order,
"Annuities" to "Will." The folders
all are new—notched in classic tri-cut,
firmly creased, neatly edged,
the old indeterminate hue.

"Start Here" comes, exceptionally, first
—a bold organizational coup:
in the folder, on a single sheet,
a bulleted list headed *"In this drawer,"*
simple annotations here and there
for ease of use ("with instructions re
disposal of remains"). A few odd items
"In the top drawer of the desk"—
"Address book," "Passport"—
fill out the bottom of the page.

This is brave, this is realism, he thinks,
yet can't quite feel it to be so.
Of course, there's more to do—
a paragraph to add, proofing to review
("disposition" of remains?).

But recently he lingers, pulled
by other tasks, less and less inspired
by the pride of doing the difficult so well,
the relief of having done. Yesterday,
hearing the final, sealing *clinch*
of the sliding metal drawer, he frowned.

Because then—a premonition—then what?
A vigil, solitary, restless, bounded by danger.
The knowledge, sliding silently into view,
that, yes, for him, when the time has come,
courage, carefulness notwithstanding,
the drawer will not be opened, the folders
never pulled, the files not perused.

Rain

It's falling heavily now, as they said it would,
in splashing thuds against the northern windows,
brutally, as if it would break and enter.
Precedence insists that it won't (I am too awake)
but brings to mind that fine, must-bearing splatter,
impossible to expunge, and those widening gaps
between glass and rattling frame above the desk—
its shaded lamp, a book left open, the day's work.

Otherwise, readiness: the pan and newspaper
where they should be on the kitchen floor,
below the puddle-shaped stain overhead,
the rolled towel against the threshold of the door—
in truth, a worn, makeshift readiness, surprised
each time by the need for a new defense, permeable
as the windows, the door, the ceiling, the roof.
The world is ending and here I lie, armed with
unwilled consciousness, wariness, calculation—prose.

When I was a boy, new rain fell like grace,
a gathering presence, unbidden, bestowing assurance,
in whispers rising nearly to song, that darkness,
silence, the reaches of the sky—the invisible and
incalculable—hold no harm, no harm at all, for you.
All is safely where it should be. Sleep.

8. CONCLUSIONS

Finishing

The love of form is a love of endings.
—Louise Glück, "Celestial Music"

What if it's somehow like the end
of a good, a well-told story?
Then you'll have completion,
have, better still, *completeness.*

The reckoning will be a rounding off,
an arrival so well foretold
by the setting forth the journey
will have seemed all along a return.

All questions will be answered.
Should the sense signal loss—
or, worse, disaster—even so,
at the sound of the last cadence,

when the long rhythms of the telling
lapse in a great easing fall
that finishes the whole,
prepare for a lift of startling fullness.

Let the speaking word ebb as it will
at the close, not hurried or slowed.
You'll feel the rightness of silence
and space.

Memorabilia

My rooms are simply furnished
but hardly austere. In the living room
stands a fine ornamental fireplace
of polished stone (the firebox sealed).
A dozen shapes enliven the mantel,
doubled by a wide backing mirror—
crystal candleholders in interesting greens,
a folded fan and delicately flowered cup
brought from Japan, a sleek Deco vase
whose birds beneath rolling clouds,
in deep cobalt, mustard, and mauve,
celebrate art's triumph over nature,
at the center a plump glass apple
inscribed, simply, *To Mr. Hathwell.*

Beside a floor lamp, above the couch,
Fred Astaire holds Rita Hayworth
in midair, Astaire cool in tie and tails,
Hayworth flinging joy, her gown blurred
by abandon. Their image hovers
unframed—nothing constrains them.

Yet how seldom these objects excite
or even catch my eye. Yes, familiarity
extinguishes (so much is invisible
because it's always there to see),
but even when I confront an object—
stare it down—how little it has to say.
(Which of these things were brought

here by others and which by me?)
If I'm stirred, to pleasure or pain,
how often it's an emotion remembered—
weightless, ghostly with nostalgia.

I could wish for a haunting.
Instead, presences quietly leave—
objects stay, stupidly, just where
I've left them. No closing of a door,
or turning of a key, summons restless
spirits of the dead. As for sounds,
the night's blank silence assures me,
when I wake to it, that I'm alone.
From the mantle the odd faint *crack:*
time's slow shifting and settling.
Nothing pitched or rhythmic,
unless it's a fumbling, a scraping,
echoing from the fireplace at nightfall,
the sound a hand must make
rummaging in an empty drawer.

NOTES ON THE POEMS

The purpose of these notes is to draw readers closer to the poems, often by clarifying allusions. They are not intended to usurp the reading experience—to tell readers how to respond to a poem. If I express hopes for a poem, I trust readers to decide for themselves if I meet them.

A poem's page number is in parentheses after its title.

1. WONDER

When Musicians Applaud (1)

Music has a unique power to overwhelm suddenly—the instant a band strikes up. Strong proof of this, for me, occurred some years ago in a small music hall with excellent acoustics. (I can't remember which.) My memory of the full orchestra's fortissimo at the start of the program, and of the musicians' "applause" at the end, inspired this poem.

Luckily, orchestral and military bands share a vocabulary. I exploit this at the close: "Recalled to their task, the *forces* rally now— / Hang poised within their *ranks* until . . ." A running ambiguity—which type of sound, primitive noise making or music making, is about to occur?—isn't resolved until the last line.

Fred's Girl (2)

It was through George Balanchine's ballet "Apollon Musagète" ("Apollo, Master of the Muses") that I learned that Apollo, Greek god of the sun, also leads the nine Muses. In the ballet, he brings the Muse of dance (and two more Muses) under his guidance. The immediate inspiration for this poem was Astaire's wonderful "master-Muse" duet with Paulette Goddard in *Second Chorus* (1940). Among Astaire's other partners in his earlier films were Ginger Rogers, Joan Leslie and Joan Fontaine, and Rita Hayworth.

The poem opens with a catalogue—a résumé—of Astaire's signature attributes, in a fifteen-line sentence of growing weight and inertia (whose one verb is *fumbled*). I want to make the reader eager for the forward-moving dance narrative that comes next. (Edmund White has called the poem "beautiful and light and stylish"—evidence that a change in tone and tempo actually occurs.)

The last paragraph takes the point of view of Fred's girl. The language turns simple and hyperbolic, as it does when we try to express ourselves in heightened states. Irving Berlin's "Cheek to Cheek," for Astaire and Rogers's *Top Hat* (1935), begins, memorably, "Heaven, I'm in heaven / And my heart beats so that I can hardly speak . . . ," on its rising musical phrase.

Poplar (5)

The language is, at first, nineteenth-century English-romantic, perhaps fulsomely so. (I summon every device for sensuous appeal I know.) Then comes the plainly analytic language through which we moderns must interpret nature now.

Wordsworth sees daffodils "Fluttering and dancing in the breeze" in a delightful "show." The spectator here experiences a double vision—that may be resolved by the notion, suggested at the close, that any enjoyment of beauty gratifies sensuous appetite and is ultimately a form of feeding.

Red Dress (7)

Jewelry (especially wedding rings) seems to challenge print advertisers to do some of their worst work.

The Day the Spaceship Landed (8)

This poem was originally dedicated to Flannery O'Connor, who specialized in small-minded characters with "flat" imaginations. Characters as smug as the woman in the poem also populate the stories of Alice Munro and Eudora Welty. But in stories by any of these writers this woman would do positive damage.

Among the inspirations for the poem was the title of Munro's story "Spaceships Have Landed" (1994). I sent the poem to Munro; she replied, "I like the poem . . . I do have a certain sympathy for the woman—perhaps because a coffee cup is my anchor through life."

2. POINTS OF VIEW

Hit the Deer (13)

This poem is based on a real event—the accidental death of a friend of my sister—but is not a strict record of what happened.

After the impersonal account of the opening stanzas, a more reflective voice considers, in the couplet, the larger ironies of situation, and then the driver's frame of mind before the accident. On the page the poem has mirror symmetry, so that as it moves on to its end, it heads back to its beginning.

Written in 2007, "Hit the Deer" was my first poem of any accomplishment. Revised in 2014, it appeared, that year, in *The Raintown Review,* a journal with "a strong bias toward formal/metrical poetry."

Shipwreck (14)

In "The Convergence of the Twain," a poem on the loss of the *Titanic,* Thomas Hardy shapes his three-line stanzas to picture a sinking ship, establishing a tradition for poets writing about nautical mishaps. With each submersion in "Shipwreck" (in the last section birds sink into light), the couplets' two lines "sink" to one. Compare "Slipping off the Raft" (page 64), where the raft stays afloat.

Readiness Is Everything (16)

About the approach of death, Hamlet says, "The readiness is all" (act 5, scene 2), and Edgar, in *King Lear,* says, "Ripeness is all" (act 5, scene 3).

Keats lived his last months in an apartment overlooking the Spanish Steps. He died there, of tuberculosis, in February 1821.

I first visited the steps as a college student, in 1962.

Sunday at the Symphony (19)

Symphonic overtures to dramatic performances, or for concert performance, were common in the nineteenth century. An instrumental "barcarole" imitates a Venetian boat song. The "seascape deemed the best" is Debussy's *La Mer.* Tchaikovsky's "grand" violin concerto is his first, opus 35.

Dust Is Winning (20)

The title bars dramatic development in the poem—it gives away how things turn out. Instead, the action is repetitive: invasion after invasion. Still, there is a progression, one of scale. I'm convinced that any reader blowing on a book as instructed would face the flurry described, and has already faced it—an assault on most of the five senses. The final siege asks the reader to imagine that little experience played out in every area of his or her most private spaces.

Dust disappears after the title—is always *it* in the poem, invisible, ubiquitous. The reader may come to feel that a still greater negative force, of entropy or disintegration, is at work.

The stanzas' jutting lines are meant to suggest shelves.

Schadenfreude (23)

The information about willowherb is drawn from a variety of creditable sources. I've made free with the sources' language, however.

My interest in willowherb dates from an interview with British writer Penelope Lively on the radio show Fresh Air in 2014. Among her most vivid childhood memories of post-blitz London, she said, is the image of "all the bombsites brimming with willowherb."

Allan Gardens (25)

Allan Gardens is a small, heavily frequented public park. The squirrel enters, and finally leaves, a visitor's field of vision.

Perhaps not so apparently, this poem is founded on classic iambic: "Sáf | er lóst | in twó | di mén | sions, súp | ple tá | il séiz | ing tó | an *S* . . ." (The first iamb is "headless.") The forward movement of its eighteen iambs is subjected to the counterrhythm of abrupt breaks and spacings.

Holding the poem at a distance, the reader might see a large *S*. The poem's design and spirit owe much to E. E. Cummings.

During Restless Sleep a Scene of Remarkable Stillness (26)

In describing this scene, I imagined a painted landscape with clearly distinguished natural elements at rising levels: lake at the bottom, then bushes, meadow, trees, and sky. The poet's job was to "paint" with latent menace.

Messenger (29)

The poem's "messenger" appears to be the herald of the strange morning moon heard at the outset, but its real messenger, and real message, aren't heard until the end.

The narrower line width is reserved for treatment of what we normally see, from our limited, earthbound perspective. The wider width is for the perspective the moon brings.

Through My Window (30)

The quotation from chapter 20 of *Middlemarch* is too long, and too good, to give in full in an epigraph: "If we had a keen vision and feeling of all ordinary human life, it would be like hearing the grass grow and the squirrel's heart beat, and we should die of that roar which lies on the other side of silence."

The narrator's improvisation riffs on familiar mythical tales of proud Greek kings (such as Midas and Sisyphus), its playful anachronisms (such as "higher-powered") perhaps suggesting the lightness and humor in Ovid. His vision of the king's punishment, however, occasions a new seriousness, and a wider paragraph that breaks past the limited frame of its surroundings.

Having little time to spare on those "figures on a well-framed stage," I hope to evoke Ezra Pound's "Petals on a wet, black bough," his stark figurative image of waiting passengers.

The setting here is from life. My study window, in San Francisco, faces the bus stop of the westbound 22 on 16th Street at Guerrero.

3. BONDS

Relativity (35)

A poem that might be called "Relationships" I call "Relativity." In truth, all that I remember of my instruction in relativity—remember vaguely at that—is the example that my high-school physics teacher offered to illustrate it. Imagine, he said, two trains moving side by side at the same speed, and you in one train able to look over at someone seated where you are (and apparently not moving) in the next—until relativity, acting only on your train, throws the trains out of sync and now, looking over, you see someone else, or no one. The transformation was meant to provoke wonder, but I, having imagined that I knew well the person lost to me, felt only appalled.

The incident recounted in the poem happened at the corner of Fifteenth and Church in San Francisco. The passenger on the southbound 22 was my husband.

Walt Whitman's great "Dalliance of the Eagles," though it describes a very different encounter, in highly charged language, nevertheless inspired the narrative contour of "Relativity," and its last line.

Orchestra, Advanced (37)

I can't play an oboe (I'm a pianist) and have never played in an orchestra (though I've sung in choruses), but two friends who played wind instruments in their high-school orchestras told me a great deal about the value of the experience.

The poem was just its first two stanzas, in much their present form—until I recognized that it couldn't end with the slapstick of the second stanza. Two years passed, however, before I was able to resolve, in a third stanza, the themes of isolation and identity raised so seriously in the first stanza.

The "hard" syllabic rhymes in the second stanza (". . . marking time until our coded cue— / then struck, bowed, plucked, or blew") are comic. The soft rhymes that conclude all three stanzas ("aimlessness . . . silences," "blew . . . day," and "sound . . . how") are not.

Voices (39), Victory (41)

"Voices" is a single utterance, its resolution delayed again and again by qualifying uncertainty. Only when the speaker believes that he's achieved understanding can the statement conclude.

My mother, Matilde Cruz Hathwell, predeceased my father,

Ernest Carlos Hathwell, by five years. I read "Victory" at a commemorative service for my father, in September 2012.

This Week's China (42)

Aunt Renée is based loosely on a beloved aunt. Bearing Aunt Marie in mind as I wrote the poem affected its development. Contrary to plan, I enter the poem, as Aunt Renée's nephew and confidant; and Aunt Renée's comic coarseness gradually softens, or at least Aunt Renée herself is regarded with increasing sympathy and affection. Bitterness, in fact, was not a hallmark of Aunt Marie's character.

Sunflower (45)

The sunflower and daisy are both in the Asteraceae family. (The aster has its own clownishness.)

"To sleep, perchance to dream" is the turning point in Hamlet's great soliloquy (act 3, scene 1).

4. THRESHOLDS

Between Dog and Wolf (49)

The French *entre chien et loup* describes moments at twilight when the eye, no longer to be trusted, can't distinguish between a dog and a wolf. The phenomenon doesn't occur every evening, or to all eyes. My most vivid experience of it, as a passenger in a car headed up Market Street in San Francisco during rush hour, inspired this poem.

The line width is often too narrow for the sense. Increasingly in each stanza, one line runs on—bounds forward—into the next. I want a careening effect, a rushing forward at increasingly reckless speed. The stanzas themselves are each a single sentence: forgoing opportunities to pause, the language only pushes ahead.

Not until I finished the poem did I recognize that its driving rhythms are measurable. It appeared in *Measure: A Review of Formal Poetry* in 2013.

Ten O'Clock (51)

Sleep science has established that, in old age, we lose the capacity to reach the deepest levels of sleep.

Freud saw dreams as media for wish fulfillment, not "dread fulfillment."

Waking at Seventy (52), Finding Myself in the Morning (55)

Though not written consecutively, these poems form a pair.

Chronologically, the last stanza of "Finding Myself in the Morning" belongs before the middle stanza. The present order shifts focus away from the gathering of the self activated by memory, toward the unoccupied state that precedes it.

Sunday Sorrow (56)

This poem began as a glib response to a friend's question, Why write poetry now? I wrote, in reply, "Beats live-in nurse / to nerves and joints / and Sunday sorrows." Later the notion of Sunday sorrow took on fuller life.

I allow myself the assumption that everyone knows what Sunday sorrow is (everyone, that is, who's had school, or work, on Monday)—knows what it feels like and when, on Sunday, it strikes.

The line widths quicken the pace of the sightings, which unfold within the continuous movement of a single sentence: "For me now / it flashes in . . ."

Gifts (59)

The line is from the third tercet of Wilbur's "Psalm," in *Anterooms* (2010): "Have the lifted horn / Greatly blare, and pronounce it / Good to have been born."

5. TRANSITIONS

Sendoff (63)

The clipped speech, in "clipped" stanzas, signals thoughtlessness and an eagerness to leave the subject.

I had Robert Browning in mind when I conceived this monologue—and the other monologues in this section. But then all dramatic monologues begin with Browning.

Slipping off the Raft (64)

Some of the lyricism of the central section is Twain-like. Why not borrow Huck Finn's peace and pleasure on his raft by allusion?

In this section, the couplet beginning "If you slip and tumble into the water, we'll all laugh . . ." is meant to lull the reader into a false sense of safety: slipping off isn't mortal (per Julia Child); it's harmless, it's fun. If the ruse works, the definitive final event will then catch the reader out.

All the couplets are self-contained except the third from last. Unstable grammatically, this couplet gives way, by elision, to the next.

The narrator may be a Charon figure, Charon being the ferryman of Hades, in Greek mythology, who transports souls from the world of the living to the world of the dead. Or may not be. It seemed wise, as I wrote this monologue, never to decide to what extent the speaker might be other than human.

Pled from the Verge (67)

This monologue, from 2013, is a kind of sequel to "The Need for Echoes" (page 75), the need there reimagined here as helpless egotism.

Irony often works by defeating expectation. The speaker's "all you had to do" promises a simple demand, not the list of wildly unreasonable requirements that follows.

This poem and Elizabeth Barrett Browning's sonnet "How do I love thee? Let me count the ways" share a glaring omission: in neither poem is any identifying quality of the person addressed evoked.

The absence of end punctuation after grammatically full statements leaves this plea "unmoored."

Pray for This (69)

To characterize dread in this poem, I use an old Christian idea that despair is hope in an unwholesome state.

I'll Be a Vessel (70)

It's easy to see that the speaker isn't seeking to be a vessel in the normal sense—isn't seeking to suppress the self to host another force, or to benefit others. Hardly. A subtler cue for irony is in "Imagine / the beauty of the scene," which I hope coaxes the reader to question the "beauty" of the condition the speaker aspires to, and the frame of mind of someone who sees it as such.

The language and its imagery may conjure Samuel Beckett, to whom this poem is informally dedicated. The poem also owes something to Shelley's "Ozymandias"—to its shifting perspective (removed, then close, then remote) and final desolation.

The vase described is in the Asian-art collection of the Denver Art Museum, in Colorado.

6. TELLING

The Need for Echoes (75)

The poet Richard Wilbur wrote, in a note to me, "'The Need for Echoes' is the sort of poem I enjoy—concretely evocative, with a clear flow of argument, and a seriousness that allows itself to be locally playful, as in 'Ecco!' The echo, in line 6, is wonderful."

The poem's "flow" has two different tempos. The rush of shuffled images in the first half gives way to a calm repetitiveness in the second. But both halves picture the reductive "canyon kind" of echo (four lines become three lines become two), and the poem is composed only of sentence fragments.

Two literary antecedents sound here, the second more remotely: Theseus's "The lunatic, the lover, and the poet . . . ," at the beginning of act 5 of *A Midsummer Night's Dream,* and E. M. Forster's *A Passage to India* and its terrible echoing caves (their nullifying "buom").

This early poem, from 2008, is at once a motto poem (a statement of why I write) and an exuberant display of a new excitement in deploying poetry's resources for communication. It began my first collection, *Muses,* as its "Call to the Reader."

Reading the Fall (76)

The waterfall described is beside a road that climbs Mount Rainier.

The two closing stanzas refer to (in this order) *The Sound and the Fury, Death of a Salesman,* Elizabeth Bishop's "The Bight," *A Streetcar Named Desire, A Passage to India,* and *The Great Gatsby.* The previous stanza begins with an allusion to Proust's *petite phrase.*

"Reading the Fall" existed first as an unpublished prose piece arguing the rewards of close reading. Recasting it in the suggestive language of verse I think doubled the power of the argument (and halved its word count).

In *Muses,* this poem was dedicated to the advanced English students I taught at Lowell High School, in San Francisco. To them I owe my best reading skills.

Song (79)

Originally called "Song of Myself," this poem is a kind of parody, though not a mocking one, of Walt Whitman's serial pantheistic identifications (in which Whitman is God, of course), the transformations occurring here at breathless, and I hope amusing, speed. The climactic stanza ("I rage against insurgents . . .") honors Whitman more directly.

Billy Collins's likable poetry is fluent and clever.

"Song" is not an earnest treatment of its subject, the act of writing poetry.

Sure Thing (81)

Poets are perhaps too tickled by metaphors' absurdity.

Do Not Use (82)

Baudelaire calls the reader his likeness (*mon semblable*) at the beginning of *Les Fleurs du Mal,* "widening gyre" is from Yeats's "The Second Coming" (the most-quarried twentieth-century lyric), and "*Write* it!" is from the climax of Elizabeth Bishop's "One Art."

Another Poem (85)

"The Circus Animals' Desertion," Yeats's poem about failing inspiration, ends, "Now that my ladder's gone, / I must lie down where all the ladders start, / In the foul rag-and-bone shop of the heart."

Family Stories (87)

In chapter 6 of Edith Wharton's *The Custom of the Country,* this is said about Undine Spragg's mother: "Mrs. Spragg liked to repeat her stories. To do so gave her almost her sole sense of permanence among the shifting scenes of her life." In this poem, repeating a story is linked to a sense of permanence derived, finally, from the shaping power of story telling.

The poem is in memory of my maternal grandfather, who immigrated to the United States, alone, from Zacatecas, Mexico, settling finally in Los Angeles, where his wife and eight children eventually joined him. Most of the details of his story are unknown to me.

Tropes (88)

John Donne's Holy Sonnet 10, "Death be not proud," ends, "One short sleep past, we wake eternally / And death shall be no more; Death, thou shalt die." The theme is biblical: "O death, where is thy sting? O grave, where is thy victory?" (1 Corinthians 15.55).

The strict, traditional formal conventions of the first half of this poem loosen in the second half.

Penned (91)

The prolific poet Donald Hall died in 2018, at ninety.

7. APPREHENSION

The Pigeon Is a Shoe (95)

My apologies to San Franciscans for the unidiomatic "Guerrero and Fourteenth." "Fourteenth and Guerrero" is local speech but has an unsatisfactory rhythm.

The events in the poem actually happened, but in reverse order: I saw the shoe (at Henry and Noe) months before I saw the cat. The more awful event has to end the poem.

Cubism (96)

Beckett presents the idea that we can't see all of anything as if it were a commonplace. It isn't one but should be, in view of its implications: we can't, of course, see what's behind us, but neither can we see what's behind what we do see.

As a representative three-dimensional object, a rectangular solid is a better choice than a cube. A cube, however, is far easier to evoke. *My* rectangular solid isn't yours, but my cube is.

The line breaks don't let the reader see the ends of statements—see them whole. The reader must track meaning around corners and across spaces. With luck, the stanzas suggest figures with three sides of differing dimensions, which is how objects—cubic or rectangular—typically appear to the eye.

The title may evoke the Cubist technique of rendering reality with the facets of solid forms, in so doing rendering it (to my eyes) baffling and uninviting.

Geology of the Sidewalk (99)

In San Francisco, squares of sidewalk needing replacement are painted by surveyors with colorful lines, Xs, and Os.

The stanzas picture three squares of sidewalk ("square by square / by square"), whose connecting borders aren't clearly demarcated grammatically.

Hidden Force Observed (101)

Our affinity for the familiar—our aversion to change, the urge to "home"—is a common subject in the social sciences (as "risk aversion," for instance) but a rare one in verse.

Among the challenges posed by my treatment: finding widely incongruous forms of experience that nevertheless re-express the notion of affinity; wording and ordering the ideas so that they feel part of a larger, accelerating movement; and sustaining the ironic tone (a silliness that doesn't entirely undercut seriousness).

If the poem's first, short utterance—its point of origin at the left margin—is home, the widening lines are steps away from home. I think of the ellipses and solecisms of the poem's second half as a sort of heedless scrambling over grammar to return home fast. To promote speed at the close, the language sheds any detaining imagery and becomes abstract.

Master of Shadows (103)

If children's books are a reliable guide, in a child's world danger is unambiguous. Villains look and act like villains; enemy creatures growl, pursue, and pounce. Adults, however, learn precautionary fear, an anxious wariness toward merely potential sources of danger, such as the master of shadows.

Built entirely on a series of questions, William Blake's "The Tyger" might nevertheless be echoed here in the questions asked in passing.

Felid and *feline* are alternative adjectives, but *felid* has no domestic associations, and no charm.

A Suit (104)

The speaker—an ordinary man, solitary, self-conscious, lacking confidence and voicing infirm resolution—may be a relative of T. S. Eliot's J. Alfred Prufrock. He declares himself "ready" to "stand up," but only "to the clerk's best blandishments."

The importance of visual detail in verse is inarguable. (It gives imagery its name.) The potential power of tactile detail—appeals to the sense of touch—may be underestimated, however.

Start Here (106)

In fact my own personal papers are not yet fully in order. (This collection represents both progress in that task and a diversion.)

Rain (109)

The childhood experience of rain appears to be unrecoverable. A natural question is why.

The poem takes place in the speaker's watchful consciousness. Most of what he sees originates in his practical imagination.

Walt Whitman's "When I Heard the Learn'd Astronomer" gives the reader a headache and then, in the conclusion, takes it away. While there is no question of headache in this poem, I attempt a similar structure. (The poems' last lines share a calmly pulsing rhythm.)

The line width allows the poem to "flood" the page.

8. CONCLUSIONS

Finishing (113)

This poem concluded *Muses,* as its "Parting Word."

Memorabilia (114)

A glass apple was presented to me by Lowell High School on the occasion of my retirement, in 2008. (I can't recall a ceremony.) In 1998, the last of my seven years at San Lorenzo High School, in the East Bay, students there gave me a clock inscribed, on a metal plaque below the clock face, "To Mr. Hathwell."

The poster of Astaire and Hayworth is an enlarged publicity photo for *You Were Never Lovelier* (1942). Another publicity photo for that film is on the cover of *Muses.*

Of the ten new poems in this collection, this one was written last. To improve the poem's coherence, the opening paragraph in early drafts (below) had to be cut—regrettably (I liked its ease). The poem, then, was called "My Room."

> It used to be a house, six or eight rooms
> casually arranged, ranch-style,
> each with its own atmosphere and view,
> its own time of day. Then time
> leveled and simplified, contracting
> the periphery until many rooms
> dwindled to a few, and now one.

ACKNOWLEDGMENTS

I am grateful to the editors of the following journals, in which the poems named first appeared, some in a slightly different form.

Angle: "Shipwreck" and "Sure Thing"

Birch Gang Review: "Cubism"

Blast Furnace: "A Suit"

California Quarterly: "Sunday Sorrow"

The Chaffin Journal: "Relativity"

Cider Press Review: "The Pigeon Is a Shoe" (also included in *Cider Press Review: Best of Volume 16*) and "Rain"

Cordite Poetry Review: "Finishing"

Driftwood Press: "Hidden Force Observed"

Into the Void: "I'll Be a Vessel"

The MacGuffin: "The Need for Echoes" and "Orchestra, Advanced"

Measure: "Between Dog and Wolf"

The Raintown Review: "Hit the Deer" and "Poplar"

Slant: "Fred's Girl," "Reading the Fall," "Slipping off the Raft," and "Through My Window"

Tampa Review: "During Restless Sleep a Scene of Remarkable Stillness" and "Pray for This"

The Timberline Review: "Dust Is Winning" and "Start Here"

"Fred's Girl" was reprinted in the *Marin Poetry Society Anthology, Volume 21* (2018).

David Robert Books published my collections *Muses* (2016) and *Between Dog and Wolf* (2017).

I am grateful, finally, to Helen Cunningham, Charles Hibbard, Staci Carney, Gary Morris, Genanne Walsh, Tina Martin, Jeffrey Escoffier, Nicole Wendel, and Jane Such for their encouragement; to Jan Camp for her unfailing talents as a designer and collaborator; and to Darcy DiNucci for her good ear and good sense.

TITLE INDEX

"M" designates a poem collected in *Muses,* "BDW" a poem collected in *Between Dog and Wolf.* Italic numbers refer to the notes.

DOG
WOLF

ABOUT THE AUTHOR

David Hathwell published *Between Dog and Wolf* in 2017 and *Muses,* his debut poetry collection, in 2016. His poems have appeared in more than a dozen literary magazines, national and international.

A former English teacher, he has a BA in English from Stanford University and an MA in English and comparative literature from Columbia University. He also holds an MA in music theory from Queens College of the City University of New York, and has studied piano at the San Francisco Conservatory of Music and sung baritone in Bay Area choruses. ("My musical training, as much as any other influence, has shaped the character of my poetry.")

He lives in San Francisco with Stephen Goldston, his partner of forty-three years and husband of eleven.

CPSIA information can be obtained
at www.ICGtesting.com
Printed in the USA
FSHW012011140619
59034FS